World War II

American history, Volume 2

Michael Johnson

Published by Harmony House Publishing, 2024.

WORLD WAR II

First edition. March 23, 2024.

Copyright © 2024 Michael Johnson.

ISBN: 979-8224543014

Written by Michael Johnson.

Table of Contents

"To the brave men and women who served and sacrificed during World War II, and to their families who endured hardship and loss, this book is dedicated. Your courage, resilience, and unwavering commitment to freedom and justice inspire us all. May your legacy live on as a testament to the triumph of the human spirit in the face of adversity. Lest we forget."

Chapter 1: The Seeds of Conflict

The interwar period between World War I and World War II was marked by a fragile peace, economic instability, and simmering tensions across the globe. As the wounds of the Great War began to heal, new challenges emerged, setting the stage for a second global conflict. In this chapter, we will delve into the complex web of global tensions that ultimately led to the outbreak of World War II, examining the economic depression, nationalism, and territorial expansion that fueled the flames of war.

1.1 The Legacy of World War I:

The end of World War I in 1918 left Europe devastated and deeply scarred. The Treaty of Versailles, signed in 1919, imposed harsh penalties on Germany, crippling its economy and stoking resentment among its people. The war's victors sought to redraw the map of Europe and reorder the global balance of power, but their efforts sowed the seeds of future conflict.

1.2 Economic Instability:

The 1920s saw a period of economic prosperity in many parts of the world, but this prosperity was built on shaky foundations. The global economy was still reeling from the effects of the war, and underlying weaknesses soon began to surface. In 1929, the stock market crash in the United States triggered the Great Depression, sending shockwaves around the world. Unemployment soared, industries collapsed, and entire economies teetered on the brink of collapse.

1.3 Rise of Totalitarianism:

Amidst the economic turmoil, a wave of political extremism swept across Europe. In Italy, Benito Mussolini rose to power, promising to restore Italy's former glory through fascism. In Germany, Adolf Hitler and the Nazi Party exploited economic hardship and nationalistic fervor to seize control, scapegoating minorities and stoking anti-Semitic sentiment. Totalitarian regimes emerged in Spain under Franco, in Japan under militarist leaders, and in the Soviet Union under Stalin, each fueling the flames of aggression and expansionism.

1.4 Nationalism and Militarism:

Nationalism, fueled by grievances from the Treaty of Versailles and exacerbated by economic hardship, became a potent force in the years leading up to World War II. Across Europe and Asia, governments tapped into feelings of national pride and resentment, promoting militarism and aggressive expansionism. Territorial disputes, unresolved by the treaties of the First World War, simmered beneath the surface, ready to erupt into open conflict.

1.5 Territorial Expansion:

The quest for territory and resources drove many nations to seek expansion beyond their borders. In Asia, Japan sought to establish a Greater East Asia Co-Prosperity Sphere, justifying its aggression with the rhetoric of Pan-Asianism. Italy invaded Ethiopia in 1935, seeking to expand its colonial empire and assert its dominance in North Africa. Meanwhile, Germany embarked on a campaign of territorial expansion, annexing Austria in 1938 and demanding the Sudetenland from Czechoslovakia in 1938.

1.6 Failure of Diplomacy:

Despite growing tensions and the specter of war looming on the horizon, diplomatic efforts to prevent conflict faltered. The policy of appeasement, pursued by Britain and France in response to German aggression, only served to embolden Hitler and reinforce his belief in the efficacy of force. The League of Nations, established in the aftermath of World War I to promote peace and collective security, proved ineffectual in the face of rising militarism and aggression.

Conclusion:

In the years leading up to World War II, the world stood on the brink of catastrophe. Economic depression, nationalism, and territorial expansion created a volatile cocktail of tensions, fueling the fires of war. Despite the lessons of the past, the international community failed to heed the warning signs, allowing old grievances to fester and new conflicts to emerge. In the next chapters, we will explore how these tensions erupted into open conflict, reshaping the course of history and altering the destiny of nations.

Chapter 2: America on the Sidelines

Amidst the growing storm clouds of war in Europe and Asia, the United States found itself initially reluctant to become embroiled in foreign conflicts. In this chapter, we will explore America's stance of isolationism, the policies that shaped its neutrality, and the events that challenged its isolationist position, ultimately leading to its entry into World War II.

2.1 America's Legacy of Isolationism:

Since its founding, the United States had maintained a tradition of avoiding entanglements in foreign affairs, a policy rooted in the belief that America's geographical isolation provided a shield from the conflicts of the Old World. This sentiment was enshrined in George Washington's Farewell Address, where he warned against "foreign entanglements" and advocated for a policy of neutrality.

2.2 The Interwar Years:

Following the devastation of World War I, America retreated into a period of introspection and retrenchment. The Senate's rejection of the Treaty of Versailles and refusal to join the League of Nations underscored America's reluctance to become involved in international affairs. Instead, the country focused on domestic concerns, enjoying a period of economic growth and cultural prosperity known as the Roaring Twenties.

2.3 The Neutrality Acts:

As tensions escalated in Europe and Asia during the 1930s, Congress passed a series of Neutrality Acts aimed at preventing the United States from being drawn into foreign conflicts. The Neutrality Act of 1935 prohibited the sale of arms to belligerent nations and imposed an arms embargo on all parties involved in a conflict. Subsequent acts in 1936 and 1937 extended these restrictions, effectively isolating America from the conflicts raging abroad.

2.4 The America First Committee:

In response to growing pressure to intervene in the European conflict, the America First Committee emerged as a vocal advocate for isolationism. Founded in 1940, the committee boasted prominent members such as aviator Charles Lindbergh and future president Gerald Ford. It organized rallies, distributed literature, and lobbied Congress to maintain America's neutrality and keep the country out of war.

2.5 The Rise of Fascism in Europe:

While America remained focused on domestic concerns, Europe was engulfed in the flames of fascism. In Italy, Benito Mussolini's fascist regime glorified militarism and sought to restore Italy's former glory. In Germany, Adolf Hitler's Nazi Party rose to power on a platform of nationalism, racism, and anti-Semitism, exploiting economic grievances and national humiliation to fuel its expansionist ambitions.

2.6 Japanese Expansion in Asia:

Meanwhile, in the Far East, Japan embarked on a campaign of imperial expansion, seeking to establish dominance over East Asia and the Pacific. The Japanese invasion of Manchuria in 1931 and subsequent aggression in China brought the United States into direct conflict with Japan, leading to deteriorating relations and a series of diplomatic crises.

2.7 Challenges to Isolationism:

Despite America's best efforts to remain aloof from foreign conflicts, events in Europe and Asia challenged its isolationist stance. The outbreak of the Spanish Civil War in 1936 and the bombing of Guernica highlighted the dangers of totalitarianism and aggression. The Anschluss of Austria in 1938 and the Munich Agreement raised concerns about appeasement and the growing threat posed by Nazi Germany.

2.8 The Fall of France:

The collapse of France in 1940 dealt a severe blow to America's isolationist illusions. With Britain standing alone against Nazi Germany, the specter of a German-dominated Europe loomed large, prompting a reassessment of America's foreign policy. President Franklin D. Roosevelt, mindful of the growing threat to American interests, began to advocate for greater preparedness and support for Britain.

2.9 Conclusion:

As the world plunged deeper into conflict, America's stance of isolationism came under increasing scrutiny. The rise of fascism in Europe and the expansion of Japan in Asia challenged America's belief in its ability to remain immune to the turmoil of the world. In the next chapter, we will explore how these challenges ultimately forced America to confront the reality of global conflict and reevaluate its role on the world stage.

Chapter 3: The Road to War

As the world teetered on the brink of war, the United States found itself increasingly drawn into the conflict despite its initial stance of isolationism. In this chapter, we will explore the shifting sentiment in America towards intervention, the pivotal events that propelled the nation towards war, and the eventual declaration of war that thrust America onto the global stage.

3.1 The Shifting Sentiment:

Throughout the late 1930s and early 1940s, public opinion in the United States underwent a dramatic transformation as events abroad forced Americans to confront the reality of global conflict. While isolationist sentiment still held sway in many quarters, growing concerns about the spread of fascism and the erosion of international order began to chip away at America's reluctance to intervene.

3.2 The Fall of France:

The fall of France in June 1940 marked a turning point in America's perception of the war. The rapid collapse of one of Europe's major powers sent shockwaves around the world, raising fears of a Nazi-dominated continent and underscoring the urgency of the situation. President Franklin D. Roosevelt, recognizing the threat posed by Nazi Germany, began to take steps to prepare America for the possibility of war.

3.3 The Battle of Britain:

As Nazi Germany turned its sights on Britain, the Battle of Britain raged in the skies over the English Channel. The heroic resistance of the British Royal Air Force against the Luftwaffe's relentless bombing campaign captured the imagination of the world and won America's admiration. The United States provided vital support to Britain through the lend-lease program, supplying weapons, ammunition, and other essential supplies to aid in its defense.

3.4 The Attack on Pearl Harbor:

On the morning of December 7, 1941, the course of American history was forever altered by a surprise attack on the naval base at Pearl Harbor, Hawaii. In a coordinated assault, Japanese aircraft launched from carriers positioned off the coast of Hawaii unleashed a devastating barrage of bombs and torpedoes, sinking or severely damaging eight battleships, three cruisers, and four destroyers. The attack claimed the lives of over 2,400 Americans and wounded thousands more, plunging the United States into war.

3.5 The Day of Infamy:

In the wake of the attack, President Franklin D. Roosevelt addressed a joint session of Congress, declaring December 7, 1941, "a date which will live in infamy." In his impassioned speech, Roosevelt called for a declaration of war against Japan and vowed that America would "win through to absolute victory." Congress responded swiftly, voting overwhelmingly to approve the president's request, with only one dissenting vote.

3.6 The Axis Powers:

The attack on Pearl Harbor thrust America into a global conflict against the Axis powers, a coalition of nations led by Germany, Italy, and Japan. The Axis powers, united by their shared commitment to fascism and militarism, posed a grave threat to the principles of democracy, freedom, and human dignity. The United States, joined by its allies, embarked on a crusade to defeat tyranny and restore peace to the world.

3.7 America Mobilizes for War:

In the aftermath of Pearl Harbor, America mobilized its vast industrial might and manpower for war. Factories retooled for wartime production, churning out tanks, planes, ships, and ammunition at an unprecedented pace. Men and women flocked to enlist in the armed forces, eager to defend their country and fight for freedom. The nation rallied behind the war effort, with slogans like "Remember Pearl Harbor" and "Loose Lips Sink Ships" becoming rallying cries for unity and resolve.

3.8 The Declaration of War:

On December 11, 1941, just four days after the attack on Pearl Harbor, Germany and Italy, in accordance with their Axis alliance with Japan, declared war on the United States. In response, Congress swiftly approved a declaration of war against Germany and Italy, cementing America's entry into World War II as a full-fledged combatant. The United States was now fully committed to the fight against tyranny and oppression on the world stage.

3.9 Conclusion:

The road to war was paved with uncertainty, fear, and sacrifice, but it was also a journey that tested the resilience and resolve of the American people. From the shock of Pearl Harbor to the declaration of war against the Axis powers,

America's entry into World War II marked a pivotal moment in history, shaping the course of the conflict and the destiny of nations. In the next chapters, we will explore America's role in the global conflict and the profound impact of the war on the nation and the world.

Chapter 4: Mobilizing the Nation

As the United States entered World War II, the nation underwent a profound transformation as it marshaled its resources and manpower for the monumental task of waging total war. In this chapter, we will explore the mobilization of American society for wartime production, the economic mobilization that fueled the war effort, and the recruitment efforts and expansion of the military that were essential to achieving victory.

4.1 The Call to Arms:

In the wake of the attack on Pearl Harbor and the subsequent declaration of war, the United States faced the daunting challenge of building a military force capable of taking on the Axis powers. President Franklin D. Roosevelt issued a call to arms, calling on all Americans to contribute to the war effort in whatever way they could. From the factories of the industrial heartland to the farms of rural America, every sector of society was mobilized for war.

4.2 Transforming American Society:

The mobilization for war brought about a fundamental shift in American society as the nation geared up for total war. Factories that had once produced consumer goods were quickly converted to wartime production, churning out tanks, planes, ships, and ammunition at an unprecedented rate. Women entered the workforce in large numbers, taking on jobs traditionally held by men who had gone off to fight. The war effort became a shared endeavor, uniting Americans from all walks of life in a common cause.

4.3 Economic Mobilization:

At the heart of America's war effort was its ability to mobilize its vast economic resources for the fight. The government implemented a series of measures to harness the power of the economy, including price controls, rationing, and the allocation of resources to key industries. The War Production Board, established in 1942, coordinated the conversion of civilian industries to wartime production and ensured a steady supply of essential materials for the military.

4.4 Role of Industries:

American industries played a central role in the war effort, producing the weapons, equipment, and supplies needed to support the military. The automobile industry, for example, retooled its factories to produce tanks, jeeps, and other military vehicles, while the aircraft industry ramped up production of fighter planes, bombers, and transport aircraft. Shipyards along the coasts churned out Liberty ships and other vessels to support the war effort on the seas.

4.5 Recruitment Efforts:

With millions of men and women joining the armed forces, recruitment efforts became a top priority for the government and military. The Selective Service System, established in 1940, drafted millions of men into military service, while recruitment campaigns encouraged volunteers to enlist in the Army, Navy, Marines, and Coast Guard. Posters, radio broadcasts, and films promoted patriotism and encouraged Americans to do their part for the war effort.

4.6 Expansion of the Military:

As the war progressed, the United States rapidly expanded its military forces to meet the demands of combat on multiple fronts. The Army, which had been relatively small prior to the war, swelled in size as millions of men were drafted or volunteered for service. The Navy expanded its fleet to protect vital sea lanes and project American power around the world. The Army Air Forces grew into a formidable fighting force, conducting bombing raids over Europe and the Pacific.

4.7 Challenges and Innovations:

The mobilization of the nation for war presented numerous challenges, from shortages of raw materials to the need for skilled labor. To overcome these challenges, American industries embraced innovation and efficiency, implementing new production techniques and technologies to increase output and reduce costs. Mass production methods pioneered by Henry Ford and others were adapted for wartime use, allowing for the rapid production of weapons and equipment on a massive scale.

4.8 The Home Front:

While the focus of the war effort was on the battlefield, the home front played a vital role in supporting the military and sustaining morale. Civilians contributed to the war effort through victory gardens, scrap metal drives, and bond sales, while communities organized war bond rallies, USO dances, and other events to boost morale and support the troops. The war effort became a unifying force, bringing Americans together in a common cause.

4.9 Conclusion:

The mobilization of the nation for war was a Herculean effort that transformed American society and propelled the United States to victory in World War II. From the factories of the industrial heartland to the farms of rural America, every sector of society played a part in the war effort, contributing to the defeat of tyranny and the defense of freedom. In the next chapters, we will explore America's role in the global conflict and the impact of the war on the nation and the world.

Chapter 5: The Pacific Theater

The Pacific Theater of World War II was a sprawling battleground spanning thousands of miles of ocean and countless islands. It was a theater of fierce naval battles, grueling amphibious assaults, and brutal jungle warfare. In this chapter, we will delve into the key battles of the Pacific Theater, the island-hopping strategy employed by Allied forces, and the pivotal role played by leaders such as Admiral Chester Nimitz and General Douglas MacArthur in shaping American strategy.

5.1 The Strategic Importance of the Pacific Theater:

The Pacific Theater was of vital strategic importance to both the Allies and the Axis powers. Control of the Pacific Ocean was essential for securing supply lines, projecting power, and protecting vital territories. For Japan, expansion into the Pacific offered access to crucial resources and the opportunity to establish a defensive perimeter against potential Allied counterattacks. For the United States, the Pacific Theater represented a gateway to Asia and the Pacific, as well as a vital lifeline to its allies in the region.

5.2 Key Battles:

5.2.1 Battle of Midway (June 1942):

The Battle of Midway was a turning point in the Pacific War, where American forces dealt a decisive blow to the Japanese Navy. Thanks to intelligence efforts and code-breaking, Admiral Chester Nimitz anticipated the Japanese attack on the Midway Atoll and positioned his forces for a preemptive strike. In a fierce battle fought primarily in the air, American dive bombers and torpedo planes sank four Japanese aircraft carriers, crippling Japan's carrier force and shifting the balance of power in the Pacific.

5.2.2 Battle of Guadalcanal (August 1942 - February 1943):

The Battle of Guadalcanal was the first major offensive by Allied forces against Japanese-held territory in the Pacific. The campaign, which began with a surprise amphibious landing on the island of Guadalcanal, quickly descended into a grueling six-month-long slog through dense jungle and brutal combat. Despite fierce Japanese resistance and harsh conditions, American and Allied forces ultimately prevailed, securing a crucial foothold in the Solomon Islands and turning the tide of the war in the Pacific.

5.2.3 Battle of Iwo Jima (February - March 1945):

The Battle of Iwo Jima was one of the bloodiest and most iconic battles of the Pacific War. American forces launched a massive amphibious assault on the heavily fortified island of Iwo Jima, seeking to capture its strategic airfields and deny Japan a staging ground for attacks on Allied bombers. The battle, fought amid rugged terrain and intense Japanese resistance, resulted in heavy casualties on both sides. Despite the high cost, American forces succeeded in capturing the island after weeks of ferocious fighting.

5.3 Island-Hopping Strategy:

The island-hopping strategy was a key element of Allied strategy in the Pacific Theater, devised by Admiral Chester Nimitz and implemented by Allied forces under the overall command of General Douglas MacArthur. Instead of attempting to capture every Japanese-held island in the Pacific, Allied forces focused on seizing key strategic objectives that would allow them to bypass heavily defended positions and advance towards Japan. This strategy, combined with naval and aerial superiority, allowed Allied forces to rapidly advance across the Pacific while minimizing casualties.

5.4 The Role of Admiral Nimitz and General MacArthur:

Admiral Chester Nimitz and General Douglas MacArthur played instrumental roles in shaping American strategy and leading Allied forces to victory in the Pacific Theater. As Commander-in-Chief of the Pacific Fleet, Nimitz oversaw naval operations and directed Allied forces in key battles such as Midway and Guadalcanal. His tactical brilliance and leadership skills were instrumental in turning the tide of the war against Japan.

General Douglas MacArthur, meanwhile, commanded Allied forces in the Southwest Pacific Theater and spearheaded the island-hopping campaign across the Pacific. Known for his bold and aggressive leadership style, MacArthur led Allied forces to victory in campaigns such as the liberation of the Philippines and the reconquest of New Guinea. His leadership and strategic vision played a crucial role in securing Allied victory in the Pacific.

5.5 Significance of the Pacific Theater:

The Pacific Theater played a pivotal role in shaping American strategy and determining the outcome of World War II. The battles fought in the Pacific were some of the largest and most ferocious of the war, with enormous casualties on both sides. The island-hopping strategy employed by Allied forces allowed them to bypass heavily fortified positions and advance towards Japan, ultimately leading to the defeat of the Axis powers in the Pacific.

5.6 Conclusion:

The Pacific Theater was a crucible of conflict that tested the resolve and courage of Allied forces in some of the most challenging conditions of the war. The key battles of Midway, Guadalcanal, and Iwo Jima, along with the island-hopping strategy and the leadership of Admiral Nimitz and General MacArthur, were instrumental in securing Allied victory in the Pacific and bringing an end to World War II. In the next chapters, we will explore the Allied campaign in the European Theater and the final defeat of Nazi Germany.

Chapter 6: The European Theater

The European Theater of World War II was the epicenter of the conflict, where the fate of nations hung in the balance and the course of history was decided on the battlefields of Europe. In this chapter, we will delve into the major campaigns that shaped the European Theater, the remarkable feats of Allied cooperation, and the harrowing atrocities of the Holocaust that cast a dark shadow over the continent.

6.1 Major Campaigns:

6.1.1 Operation Overlord (D-Day):

Operation Overlord, commonly known as D-Day, was the largest amphibious invasion in history and a turning point in World War II. On June 6, 1944, Allied forces launched a massive assault on the beaches of Normandy, France, with the aim of establishing a beachhead and opening a second front against Nazi Germany. Despite heavy casualties and fierce German resistance, Allied forces succeeded in securing the beachheads and beginning the liberation of Western Europe.

6.1.2 Battle of Stalingrad:

The Battle of Stalingrad was one of the deadliest battles of World War II and a turning point in the Eastern Front. Fought from August 1942 to February 1943, the battle saw German forces launch a massive offensive to capture the city of Stalingrad, a key strategic objective on the road to Moscow. The battle devolved into brutal urban combat, with street-to-street fighting and hand-to-hand combat in the ruins of the city. In the end, Soviet forces emerged victorious, inflicting massive casualties on the German army and dealing a severe blow to Hitler's war machine.

6.1.3 Battle of the Bulge:

The Battle of the Bulge was the last major German offensive on the Western Front and one of the largest battles of World War II. Launched in December 1944, the offensive aimed to split the Allied lines, recapture the port of Antwerp, and force the Allies to negotiate a separate peace. The surprise attack caught the Allies off guard, leading to fierce fighting in the dense Ardennes Forest. Despite initial setbacks, Allied forces rallied and repelled the German advance, ultimately turning the tide of the battle and hastening the end of the war in Europe.

6.2 Allied Cooperation:

The success of the Allied campaign in Europe was built on a foundation of unprecedented cooperation and collaboration between the Allied powers. The United States, Great Britain, and the Soviet Union, despite their differences and competing interests, worked together to defeat Nazi Germany and liberate Europe from tyranny.

6.2.1 Leadership of Eisenhower:

General Dwight D. Eisenhower, as Supreme Commander of the Allied Expeditionary Force, played a central role in coordinating Allied operations in Europe. Eisenhower's strategic vision, leadership skills, and ability to forge consensus among Allied leaders were instrumental in the success of Operation Overlord and the subsequent campaign in Western Europe. His steady hand and unwavering determination inspired confidence and unity among Allied forces.

6.2.2 Leadership of Churchill:

Winston Churchill, the Prime Minister of Great Britain, was a towering figure in Allied leadership and a staunch advocate for the defeat of Nazi Germany. Churchill's eloquence, resolve, and indomitable spirit rallied the British people and inspired the Allied cause during the darkest days of the war. His partnership with President Franklin D. Roosevelt and Soviet Premier Joseph Stalin formed the backbone of Allied cooperation and laid the groundwork for victory in Europe.

6.3 Liberation of Concentration Camps:

As Allied forces advanced across Europe, they encountered the horrifying reality of Nazi atrocities and the systematic genocide of millions of innocent civilians. The liberation of concentration camps such as Auschwitz, Bergen-Belsen, and Dachau exposed the full extent of Nazi brutality and shocked the world's conscience.

6.3.1 Horrors of the Holocaust:

The Holocaust, perpetrated by the Nazis during World War II, remains one of the darkest chapters in human history. Six million Jews, along with millions of others deemed undesirable by the Nazis, including Romani people, disabled individuals, political dissidents, and homosexuals, were systematically murdered in gas chambers, mass shootings, and other atrocities. The liberation of the concentration camps by Allied forces brought an end to the horrors of the Holocaust but left an indelible mark on the world's collective memory.

6.4 Conclusion:

The European Theater of World War II was a crucible of conflict that tested the resolve and courage of Allied forces in the fight against tyranny and oppression. The major campaigns such as Operation Overlord, the Battle of Stalingrad, and the Battle of the Bulge, along with the remarkable feats of Allied cooperation and the liberation of concentration camps, shaped the course of history and laid the groundwork for a new era of peace and prosperity in Europe. In the next chapters, we will explore the aftermath of World War II and its lasting impact on the world.

Chapter 7: The Home Front

The home front during World War II was a time of profound transformation and sacrifice for the American people. As the nation mobilized for war, every aspect of life was affected, from the economy and industry to society and culture. In this chapter, we will explore the experiences of Americans on the home front, including rationing, propaganda, and the role of women in the workforce, as well as the social changes and challenges faced by minorities, and the impact of government policies on civil liberties and American society.

7.1 Life on the Home Front:

7.1.1 Rationing:

With the onset of war, the United States government implemented rationing programs to ensure that essential goods such as food, fuel, and textiles were fairly distributed and conserved for the war effort. Ration books were issued to every household, containing coupons that limited the amount of goods individuals could purchase. Items such as meat, sugar, coffee, and gasoline were rationed, leading to changes in consumer habits and the development of recipes that made do with limited ingredients.

7.1.2 Propaganda:

Propaganda played a crucial role in mobilizing public support for the war effort and shaping public opinion on the home front. Through posters, films, radio broadcasts, and other media, the government sought to instill a sense of patriotism, unity, and sacrifice among the American people. Propaganda campaigns promoted themes of duty, sacrifice, and victory, while demonizing the enemy and rallying support for the war.

7.1.3 Women in the Workforce:

As millions of men enlisted in the armed forces and went off to fight, women stepped into the workforce in unprecedented numbers to fill the labor shortages left behind. Women took on jobs in factories, shipyards, and munitions plants, producing weapons, ammunition, and other essential war materials. The iconic image of "Rosie the Riveter" became a symbol of the contributions of women to the war effort and paved the way for greater opportunities and recognition in the workforce.

7.2 Social Changes and Challenges Faced by Minorities:

7.2.1 African Americans:

For African Americans, the war presented both opportunities and challenges. While the war effort created new job opportunities in industries such as defense production, discrimination and segregation persisted in many aspects of life. African American soldiers served with distinction in segregated units, facing discrimination both at home and abroad. The war also provided a catalyst for the Civil Rights Movement, as African Americans demanded equal rights and opportunities in the military and on the home front.

7.2.2 Japanese Americans:

The internment of Japanese Americans during World War II remains one of the darkest chapters in American history. In the wake of the attack on Pearl Harbor, thousands of Japanese Americans, many of them citizens, were forcibly removed from their homes and incarcerated in internment camps under Executive Order 9066. The internment of Japanese Americans violated their civil liberties and constitutional rights, and had lasting impacts on individuals and families.

7.2.3 Native Americans:

Native Americans made significant contributions to the war effort, serving in the armed forces and working in industries critical to the war effort. Native American code talkers played a vital role in transmitting coded messages that were impossible for the enemy to decipher. Despite their contributions, Native Americans faced discrimination and marginalization both during and after the war, as they continued to fight for recognition of their rights and sovereignty.

7.3 Civil Liberties and Government Policies:

7.3.1 Executive Order 9066:

Executive Order 9066, issued by President Franklin D. Roosevelt in February 1942, authorized the internment of Japanese Americans and individuals of Japanese descent living on the West Coast. Under the order, over 120,000 Japanese Americans, including men, women, and children, were forcibly removed from their homes and incarcerated in internment camps for the duration of the war. The internment of Japanese Americans remains a dark chapter in American history and a violation of civil liberties.

7.3.2 War Powers and Civil Liberties:

The war effort also led to an expansion of government powers and restrictions on civil liberties in the name of national security. Measures such as censorship, surveillance, and the suspension of habeas corpus were implemented to protect against espionage and sabotage. While these measures were intended to safeguard the nation, they also raised concerns about the erosion of civil liberties and the potential for abuse of power.

7.3.3 Legacy of the Home Front:

The experiences of Americans on the home front during World War II had a profound impact on American society and culture. The war brought about significant social and economic changes, including the expansion of women's roles in the workforce, the advancement of civil rights, and the growth of the federal government's role in the economy and society. The legacy of the home front continues to shape American society and politics to this day, serving as a reminder of the sacrifices and resilience of the Greatest Generation.

Chapter 8: War and Diplomacy

World War II not only reshaped the global landscape through military conflict but also laid the groundwork for a new world order through diplomacy and international cooperation. In this chapter, we will explore the pivotal Allied conferences at Tehran, Yalta, and Potsdam, examine the role of diplomacy in shaping the post-war world, and discuss the establishment of the United Nations and its vision for a new international order.

8.1 Tehran Conference (1943):

The Tehran Conference, held from November 28 to December 1, 1943, marked the first meeting between the "Big Three" Allied leaders: Joseph Stalin of the Soviet Union, Franklin D. Roosevelt of the United States, and Winston Churchill of Great Britain. The conference focused on strategic planning for the remainder of the war and the coordination of military efforts against Nazi Germany.

Key outcomes of the Tehran Conference included the agreement to launch Operation Overlord, the Allied invasion of Normandy, in 1944, and the establishment of the European Advisory Commission to plan for the post-war occupation and reconstruction of Europe. The conference also laid the groundwork for future Allied cooperation and set the stage for subsequent conferences at Yalta and Potsdam.

8.2 Yalta Conference (1945):

The Yalta Conference, held from February 4 to 11, 1945, brought together Stalin, Roosevelt, and Churchill for a second time to discuss the post-war reorganization of Europe and the establishment of a new world order. The conference took place as Allied forces were advancing on Nazi Germany from both the east and the west, and the defeat of Germany seemed imminent.

At Yalta, the Allied leaders reached agreements on a number of key issues, including the division of Germany into occupation zones, the establishment of the United Nations, and the organization of free elections in liberated European countries. However, disagreements over the future of Poland and Eastern Europe foreshadowed tensions that would emerge in the post-war period.

8.3 Potsdam Conference (1945):

The Potsdam Conference, held from July 17 to August 2, 1945, marked the final meeting between the leaders of the Big Three Allied powers. By this time, Germany had surrendered, and the focus of the conference shifted to the reconstruction of Europe and the ongoing war against Japan.

Key outcomes of the Potsdam Conference included the agreement to demilitarize Germany, disarm its armed forces, and put Nazi war criminals on trial. The conference also addressed the future of Eastern Europe, with agreements reached on the borders of Poland and the expulsion of Germans from territories east of the Oder-Neisse line.

8.4 The Role of Diplomacy:

Diplomacy played a central role in shaping the post-war world order and laying the groundwork for peace and stability in the aftermath of World War II. Through negotiations, agreements, and alliances, the Allied powers sought to rebuild Europe, promote democracy, and prevent the recurrence of another global conflict.

Diplomacy also played a crucial role in managing the emerging Cold War tensions between the United States and the Soviet Union, as competing ideologies and geopolitical interests clashed in the aftermath of World War II. The division of Germany and the establishment of the Iron Curtain in Eastern Europe marked the beginning of a new era of global competition and confrontation.

8.5 The United Nations:

One of the most significant outcomes of the Allied conferences was the establishment of the United Nations, an international organization founded to promote peace, security, and cooperation among nations. The United Nations Charter, signed at the San Francisco Conference in 1945, outlined the organization's principles and objectives, including the maintenance of international peace and security, the promotion of human rights, and the settlement of disputes through peaceful means.

The United Nations represented a departure from the isolationism and unilateralism of the interwar period, signaling a commitment to collective security and multilateral cooperation in addressing global challenges. While the United Nations has faced its share of challenges and criticisms over the years, it remains a cornerstone of the international order and a forum for dialogue and diplomacy among nations.

8.6 Vision for a New International Order:

The Allied conferences and the establishment of the United Nations reflected a vision for a new international order based on the principles of democracy, freedom, and cooperation. In the aftermath of World War II, the world sought to rebuild and recover from the devastation of war, while also addressing the underlying causes of conflict and instability.

The vision for a new international order included efforts to promote economic development, human rights, and self-determination, as well as to prevent the spread of nuclear weapons and ensure the peaceful resolution of disputes. While the challenges of the post-war era were immense, the commitment to collective action and cooperation paved the way for a more peaceful and prosperous world.

8.7 Conclusion:

The Allied conferences of Tehran, Yalta, and Potsdam, along with the establishment of the United Nations, were pivotal moments in shaping the post-war world order and laying the groundwork for peace and stability in the aftermath of World War II. Through diplomacy, negotiation, and cooperation, the Allied powers sought to rebuild Europe, promote democracy, and prevent the recurrence of another global conflict. While the challenges of the post-war era were immense, the vision for a new international order represented a commitment to collective action and cooperation in addressing the challenges of the modern world.

Chapter 9: Technology and Innovation

World War II was a conflict that propelled humanity into an era of unprecedented technological innovation. From advances in weaponry and communication to breakthroughs in medicine and engineering, the war spurred rapid developments that would shape the course of history. In this chapter, we will explore the pivotal role of technology in shaping the outcome of the war, examine the key advances in weaponry, communication, and medicine, and discuss the legacy of wartime innovation in post-war America.

9.1 The Role of Technology in Shaping the Outcome of the War:

Technology played a crucial role in determining the outcome of World War II, influencing strategies, tactics, and the balance of power on the battlefield. Innovations in weapons, transportation, communication, and logistics transformed the nature of warfare and gave advantage to those nations that could harness these technologies effectively.

9.1.1 Weapons Technology:

Advances in weapons technology revolutionized the way wars were fought during World War II. The development of tanks, aircraft, artillery, and small arms resulted in unprecedented destruction and casualties on the battlefield. Innovations such as the tank blitzkrieg, precision bombing, and amphibious assaults reshaped military doctrine and strategy, while the introduction of radar, sonar, and code-breaking techniques gave Allied forces crucial advantages in intelligence and reconnaissance.

9.1.2 Communication Technology:

Communication technology played a vital role in coordinating military operations and maintaining command and control on the battlefield. The use of radio, telegraph, and encrypted communication systems enabled commanders to coordinate movements, relay orders, and gather intelligence in real-time. Advances in cryptography and code-breaking, such as the British breaking of the German Enigma code, gave Allied forces crucial insights into enemy plans and intentions.

9.1.3 Medical Technology:

Medical technology made significant strides during World War II, saving countless lives and alleviating suffering on the battlefield. Innovations such as blood transfusions, antibiotics, and surgical techniques helped to improve survival rates among wounded soldiers and reduce the spread of infectious diseases. Mobile field hospitals and evacuation systems enabled medical personnel to provide rapid and effective care to casualties, while advances in prosthetics and rehabilitation helped injured veterans to recover and reintegrate into civilian life.

9.2 Advances in Weaponry:

9.2.1 Tanks:

The development of tanks played a crucial role in World War II, transforming the nature of land warfare and providing armored firepower on the battlefield. Tanks such as the German Panzer, the American Sherman, and the Soviet T-34 became iconic symbols of military might and innovation, with each nation racing to develop faster, more heavily armored, and more powerful tanks to gain an edge over their adversaries.

9.2.2 Aircraft:

Aircraft played a decisive role in World War II, providing air superiority, close air support, and strategic bombing capabilities to the warring nations. Technological advances such as the jet engine, radar, and guided missiles revolutionized aerial warfare, allowing for faster speeds, greater range, and more precise targeting. Iconic aircraft such as the British Spitfire, the American B-17 Flying Fortress, and the German Messerschmitt Bf 109 became synonymous with the air war over Europe and the Pacific.

9.2.3 Naval Warfare:

Naval warfare saw significant technological advancements during World War II, with the development of aircraft carriers, submarines, and amphibious assault ships revolutionizing naval tactics and strategy. Aircraft carriers such as the American USS Enterprise and the Japanese Akagi became the centerpiece of naval operations, projecting air power across vast distances and dominating the seas. Submarines, armed with torpedoes and guided missiles, wreaked havoc on enemy shipping lanes and disrupted supply lines, while amphibious assault ships enabled Allied forces to launch large-scale invasions of enemy-held territories.

9.3 Advances in Communication:

9.3.1 Radar:

Radar technology played a crucial role in World War II, providing early warning of enemy aircraft, ships, and ground forces. Radar stations located along coastlines and on ships could detect and track incoming threats, allowing for rapid response and interception by fighter aircraft and anti-aircraft defenses. Radar also played a key role in navigation and targeting, enabling precision bombing and artillery fire against enemy positions.

9.3.2 Encryption and Code-Breaking:

Encryption and code-breaking were critical components of military communication during World War II, with both Allied and Axis powers employing sophisticated cryptographic systems to encode and decode messages. The British breaking of the German Enigma code, a feat accomplished by the code-breakers at Bletchley Park, provided Allied forces with crucial intelligence and insights into German military plans and intentions. Similarly, Axis code-breaking efforts, such as the Japanese breaking of American codes at Pearl Harbor, enabled surprise attacks and strategic deception.

9.3.3 Radio and Telecommunications:

Radio and telecommunications played a vital role in coordinating military operations and maintaining command and control on the battlefield. Portable radios, walkie-talkies, and field telephones enabled soldiers to communicate with their commanders and coordinate movements in real-time, while long-range radio transmissions facilitated communication between headquarters and frontline units. Radio broadcasts and propaganda campaigns also played a crucial role in shaping public opinion and morale on the home front.

9.4 Advances in Medicine:

9.4.1 Blood Transfusion:

Blood transfusion technology made significant advancements during World War II, enabling medical personnel to provide rapid and effective treatment to wounded soldiers on the battlefield. The development of blood banks, refrigerated storage, and blood typing techniques allowed for the safe and efficient transfusion of blood and plasma to casualties, reducing the risk of infection and improving survival rates.

9.4.2 Antibiotics:

The discovery and widespread use of antibiotics revolutionized the treatment of infectious diseases and wound infections during World War II. Drugs such as penicillin, streptomycin, and sulfa drugs proved highly effective in combating bacterial infections and preventing the spread of disease among wounded soldiers. The availability of antibiotics on the battlefield saved countless lives and helped to reduce the morbidity and mortality associated with infectious diseases.

9.4.3 Surgical Techniques:

Advances in surgical techniques and anesthesia played a crucial role in treating traumatic injuries and performing lifesaving surgeries on the battlefield. Innovations such as the use of sterile techniques, blood transfusions, and anesthesia enabled surgeons to perform complex procedures under challenging conditions, resulting in improved outcomes and reduced mortality rates among wounded soldiers. Mobile field hospitals, equipped with operating theaters and medical supplies, provided frontline medical care to casualties and facilitated rapid evacuation and treatment of the wounded.

9.5 The Legacy of Wartime Innovation in Post-War America:

The legacy of wartime innovation in World War II had a profound and lasting impact on American society and culture, shaping the course of technological development and economic growth in the post-war era. The technological advances made during the war laid the groundwork for new industries and technologies that would transform everyday life and drive innovation in the decades to come.

9.5.1 Economic Growth:

The wartime mobilization effort stimulated economic growth and industrial expansion in the United States, laying the foundation for the post-war economic boom. The massive investments in defense production and infrastructure during World War II spurred innovation and productivity gains across a wide range of industries, from manufacturing and construction to transportation and telecommunications. The influx of government funding and the demand for goods and services created millions of new jobs and fueled consumer spending, driving economic growth and prosperity in the post-war years.

9.5.2 Technological Innovation:

The technological innovations of World War II laid the groundwork for new industries and technologies that would shape the modern world. Advances in aviation, electronics, telecommunications, and medicine spurred innovation and entrepreneurship, leading to breakthroughs such as the development of commercial aviation, the proliferation of television and radio broadcasting, and the widespread adoption of antibiotics and other medical treatments. The wartime research and development efforts also paved the way for future innovations in fields such as computer science, aerospace engineering, and biomedical research, fueling a new era of technological progress and innovation.

9.5.3 Scientific Research:

World War II also accelerated scientific research and discovery, leading to groundbreaking advances in physics, chemistry, and biology. The development of atomic weapons, radar technology, and electronic computing relied on the contributions of scientists and researchers from around the world, many of whom went on to make significant contributions to post-war science and technology. The wartime collaboration between government, industry, and academia laid the foundation for future scientific breakthroughs and established the United States as a global leader in scientific research and innovation.

9.5.4 Social and Cultural Impact:

The legacy of wartime innovation extended beyond the realm of technology and economics, influencing social attitudes and cultural norms in post-war America. The wartime experience fostered a spirit of patriotism, unity, and shared sacrifice among the American people, shaping the collective memory of the war and its significance in shaping the nation's identity. The contributions of women, minorities, and immigrants to the war effort challenged traditional gender and racial roles, paving the way for greater social equality and inclusion in post-war society. The legacy of wartime innovation also inspired a new generation of entrepreneurs, inventors, and innovators who sought to build upon the achievements of the past and create a better future for themselves and their communities.

9.6 Conclusion:

The technological innovations of World War II transformed the course of history, shaping the outcome of the war and laying the groundwork for a new era of prosperity and progress in the post-war world. From advances in weaponry and communication to breakthroughs in medicine and engineering, the wartime innovations of World War II revolutionized the way wars were fought and paved the way for new industries and technologies that would shape the modern world. The legacy of wartime innovation continues to resonate today, serving as a testament to the ingenuity, resilience, and determination of the Greatest Generation and their enduring impact on the world we live in.

Chapter 10: The Homecoming

The end of World War II marked a moment of relief and celebration for millions of servicemen and women who had endured the hardships and horrors of combat. However, the return to civilian life posed its own set of challenges, as veterans grappled with the transition from military service to civilian society. In this chapter, we will explore the challenges of demobilization and returning to civilian life, examine the transformative impact of the GI Bill on education, housing, and employment, and discuss veterans' experiences and the lasting effects of war trauma.

10.1 The Challenges of Demobilization:

The demobilization of millions of servicemen and women at the end of World War II presented a logistical and social challenge of unprecedented scale. The transition from military service to civilian life required adjusting to new routines, roles, and responsibilities, as well as reconnecting with family, friends, and communities. For many veterans, the return home was bittersweet, marked by feelings of pride, relief, and gratitude, as well as a sense of dislocation, loss, and uncertainty about the future.

10.1.1 Reintegration into Civilian Society:

The process of reintegration into civilian society was often fraught with challenges, as veterans struggled to readjust to civilian life after months or years of military service. Many veterans experienced difficulties finding employment, securing housing, and accessing healthcare and social services, leading to feelings of frustration, isolation, and disillusionment. The stigma and misconceptions surrounding mental health and war trauma also made it difficult for veterans to seek help and support for their emotional and psychological needs.

10.1.2 Economic Challenges:

The transition from military service to civilian life posed significant economic challenges for veterans, many of whom faced unemployment, underemployment, or financial hardship upon returning home. The post-war economy experienced periods of inflation, shortages, and economic uncertainty, making it difficult for veterans to find stable employment and provide for themselves and their families. The loss of wartime wages and benefits also put additional strain on veterans' finances, exacerbating existing economic disparities and inequalities.

10.1.3 Social Reintegration:

The social reintegration of veterans into civilian life was often complicated by the psychological and emotional toll of war trauma, as well as the challenges of readjusting to civilian norms and expectations. Many veterans struggled with feelings of alienation, guilt, and survivor's guilt, as well as difficulties forming and maintaining relationships with family, friends, and peers. The stigma surrounding mental health and war trauma further compounded veterans' sense of isolation and shame, making it difficult for them to seek help and support from others.

10.2 The GI Bill and Its Impact:

The Servicemen's Readjustment Act of 1944, commonly known as the GI Bill, was a landmark piece of legislation that provided a comprehensive package of benefits and support to returning World War II veterans. The GI Bill aimed to ease the transition to civilian life, promote economic opportunity, and support veterans in pursuing their educational and career goals. The impact of the GI Bill was transformative, revolutionizing access to education, homeownership, and employment for millions of veterans and their families.

10.2.1 Education Benefits:

One of the most significant provisions of the GI Bill was its education benefits, which provided funding for veterans to pursue higher education and vocational training. Under the GI Bill, veterans could receive financial assistance for tuition, fees, books, and supplies, as well as a monthly living stipend to cover housing and living expenses. This unprecedented investment in veterans' education opened up new opportunities for advancement and upward mobility, allowing veterans to acquire the skills and qualifications needed to succeed in civilian careers.

10.2.2 Homeownership Benefits:

The GI Bill also included provisions to help veterans purchase homes and access affordable housing. Through the VA Home Loan Guaranty Program, veterans could obtain low-interest mortgages with no down payment, enabling them to buy homes with favorable terms and build wealth through homeownership. The VA loan program helped millions of veterans and their families achieve the dream of homeownership, expand the middle class, and stimulate economic growth and development in communities across the country.

10.2.3 Employment Assistance:

In addition to education and housing benefits, the GI Bill provided employment assistance and job training programs to help veterans find and retain employment in the civilian workforce. The Veterans' Employment Service (VES) offered career counseling, job placement services, and vocational training programs tailored to veterans' skills and interests, helping them transition smoothly from military service to civilian employment. The GI Bill also incentivized employers to hire veterans by offering tax credits and other financial incentives, encouraging businesses to prioritize veterans' employment and support their reintegration into the workforce.

10.3 Veterans' Experiences and the Lasting Effects of War Trauma:

Despite the support provided by the GI Bill and other programs, many veterans continued to struggle with the physical, emotional, and psychological toll of war trauma long after returning home. The experiences of combat, loss, and trauma left lasting scars on veterans' minds and bodies, shaping their attitudes, behaviors, and relationships for years to come. The stigma surrounding mental health and war trauma made it difficult for veterans to seek help and support, leading many to suffer in silence and isolation.

10.3.1 Psychological and Emotional Challenges:

Many veterans experienced a range of psychological and emotional challenges as a result of their wartime experiences, including post-traumatic stress disorder (PTSD), depression, anxiety, and survivor's guilt. The symptoms of war trauma, such as nightmares, flashbacks, hypervigilance, and emotional numbness, could be debilitating and disruptive to veterans' daily lives, making it difficult for them to function effectively and maintain stable relationships and employment.

10.3.2 Physical Disabilities and Injuries:

In addition to psychological and emotional challenges, many veterans also grappled with physical disabilities and injuries sustained in combat. Wounded veterans faced long and arduous recoveries, as well as ongoing medical treatments, surgeries, and rehabilitation programs to help them regain their mobility and independence. Physical disabilities such as limb loss, traumatic brain injuries, and chronic pain often required lifelong care and support, posing significant challenges to veterans' ability to work, socialize, and participate fully in community life. The physical and emotional toll of war injuries and disabilities could strain veterans' relationships with family members and caregivers, as well as their ability to navigate the complexities of the healthcare system and access the services and supports they needed to thrive.

10.3.3 Social Isolation and Alienation:

Many veterans struggled with feelings of social isolation and alienation upon returning home, as they grappled with the challenges of readjusting to civilian life and reconnecting with family, friends, and peers. The experiences of war trauma, loss, and grief could create barriers to intimacy and connection, leading veterans to withdraw from social interactions and retreat into themselves. The stigma surrounding mental health and war trauma also made it difficult for veterans to reach out for help and support, further exacerbating their sense of isolation and loneliness.

10.3.4 Substance Abuse and Addiction:

Some veterans turned to substance abuse and addiction as a way of coping with the physical and emotional pain of war trauma and readjusting to civilian life. Alcoholism, drug abuse, and prescription medication misuse were common among veterans struggling with PTSD, depression, and anxiety, as well as those grappling with chronic pain and disabilities. Substance abuse and addiction could further exacerbate veterans' mental health issues, impair their judgment and decision-making abilities, and strain their relationships with family members, friends, and employers.

10.4 The Long-Term Impact of War Trauma:

The long-term impact of war trauma on veterans and their families cannot be overstated, as it permeates every aspect of their lives and shapes their identities, relationships, and futures. War trauma can have profound and enduring effects on veterans' mental and physical health, as well as their social and economic well-being, leading to increased rates of disability, unemployment, homelessness, and suicide among veterans compared to the general population.

10.4.1 Mental Health:

War trauma can have a lasting impact on veterans' mental health, contributing to the development of psychiatric disorders such as PTSD, depression, anxiety, and substance abuse. These conditions can impair veterans' ability to function effectively in their daily lives, disrupt their relationships and social support networks, and undermine their sense of self-worth and purpose. Left untreated, mental health issues can escalate over time and lead to a range of negative outcomes, including homelessness, incarceration, and suicide.

10.4.2 Physical Health:

War trauma can also have significant effects on veterans' physical health, leading to chronic pain, disability, and medical conditions related to combat injuries and exposures. Veterans may experience a higher prevalence of conditions such as musculoskeletal disorders, traumatic brain injuries, hearing loss, and respiratory illnesses as a result of their military service. These physical health issues can exacerbate veterans' mental health problems and impair their ability to work, socialize, and engage in activities of daily living.

10.4.3 Social and Economic Well-Being:

War trauma can impact veterans' social and economic well-being, affecting their relationships, employment opportunities, and financial stability. Veterans may struggle to maintain stable housing, access healthcare and social services, and participate fully in community life due to the challenges posed by war trauma and its associated symptoms. The stigma surrounding mental health and war trauma can also create barriers to veterans' reintegration into civilian society, leading to social isolation, unemployment, and poverty.

10.5 The Role of Supportive Services and Resources:

Supportive services and resources play a crucial role in helping veterans cope with the challenges of war trauma and rebuild their lives in the aftermath of military service. Organizations such as the Department of Veterans Affairs (VA), veterans service organizations (VSOs), and community-based nonprofits offer a wide range of programs and services designed to meet veterans' unique needs and promote their health and well-being.

10.5.1 Mental Health Care:

Access to mental health care is essential for veterans struggling with war trauma and related mental health issues. The VA provides comprehensive mental health services, including counseling, therapy, medication management, and support groups, to veterans and their families. Telehealth and telemedicine programs also enable veterans to access mental health care remotely, reducing barriers to treatment and increasing access to care for those living in rural or underserved areas.

10.5.2 Disability Compensation and Benefits:

Veterans who experience service-related disabilities and injuries may be eligible for disability compensation and benefits through the VA. Disability compensation provides financial support to veterans who have disabilities that are a result of their military service, including physical injuries, mental health conditions, and other impairments. These benefits help veterans cover the costs of medical care, treatment, and rehabilitation, as well as provide financial support for themselves and their families.

10.5.3 Vocational Rehabilitation and Employment Services:

Veterans who face barriers to employment due to war trauma or service-related disabilities can receive vocational rehabilitation and employment services through the VA.These services include vocational counseling, job training, job placement assistance, and support for starting a business or pursuing self-employment. Vocational rehabilitation programs help veterans identify their skills and interests, develop job readiness skills, and explore career options that align with their abilities and goals. Employment services connect veterans with employers who value their military experience and provide accommodations and support to help them succeed in the workplace.

10.5.4 Housing Assistance:

Veterans who are homeless or at risk of homelessness can access housing assistance and supportive services through programs such as the VA's Homeless Veterans Program. These programs provide temporary housing, rental assistance, and case management services to help veterans secure stable and affordable housing. Supportive services such as counseling, substance abuse treatment, and mental health care are also available to help veterans address the underlying issues contributing to their housing instability and achieve long-term housing stability.

10.5.5 Peer Support and Peer Mentoring:

Peer support and peer mentoring programs connect veterans with peers who have similar experiences and can offer understanding, empathy, and encouragement. These programs provide opportunities for veterans to share their stories, build relationships, and learn from each other's experiences in a supportive and non-judgmental environment. Peer support and peer mentoring can help veterans feel less isolated and alone, strengthen their coping skills and resilience, and promote their overall health and well-being.

10.6 The Importance of Community Support:

Community support plays a vital role in helping veterans reintegrate into civilian life and overcome the challenges of war trauma. Local communities, faith-based organizations, and civic groups can provide valuable resources and support to veterans and their families, including peer support groups, volunteer opportunities, and social activities. By welcoming veterans into their communities with open arms and offering them support and friendship, communities can help veterans feel valued, respected, and connected to the broader community fabric.

10.6.1 Veteran-Friendly Employers:

Employers have a critical role to play in supporting veterans' successful transition to civilian employment and promoting their long-term economic stability. Veteran-friendly employers recognize the unique skills, experiences, and leadership qualities that veterans bring to the workplace and create inclusive and supportive work environments where veterans can thrive. These employers may offer military-friendly policies and benefits, such as flexible scheduling, tuition assistance, and mentorship programs, to help veterans succeed in their careers and advance professionally.

10.6.2 Military and Veteran Service Organizations:

Military and veteran service organizations (VSOs) play a crucial role in advocating for veterans' rights, providing support services, and connecting veterans with resources and benefits. Organizations such as the American Legion, Veterans of Foreign Wars (VFW), and Disabled American Veterans (DAV) offer a wide range of programs and services tailored to veterans' needs, including advocacy, representation, financial assistance, and camaraderie. VSOs also play a vital role in preserving veterans' legacies, honoring their service and sacrifices, and promoting awareness and appreciation of their contributions to the nation.

10.7 Conclusion:

The homecoming experience for veterans of World War II was a complex and multifaceted journey, marked by both triumphs and challenges as veterans navigated the transition from military service to civilian life. While the GI Bill provided unprecedented support and opportunities for returning veterans, many still faced significant barriers to reintegration, including the physical, emotional, and psychological toll of war trauma. However, through the support of supportive services, community resources, and the unwavering camaraderie of their fellow veterans, many were able to overcome these challenges and build fulfilling and meaningful lives in the post-war era. As we reflect on the sacrifices and contributions of the Greatest Generation, let us honor their legacy by ensuring that today's veterans receive the support, respect, and appreciation they deserve as they make their own journey home.

Chapter 11: Remembering the Fallen

The sacrifices of those who served in World War II are etched into the collective memory of nations around the world. From the fields of Europe to the Pacific islands, millions of servicemen and women gave their lives in the fight against tyranny and oppression. In this chapter, we will delve into the solemn task of memorializing these sacrifices, exploring the establishment of national monuments and memorials, examining commemoration ceremonies, and discussing the cultural legacy of World War II.

11.1 Memorializing the Sacrifices:

The enormity of the human cost of World War II demanded a profound and lasting tribute to those who made the ultimate sacrifice. Across the globe, communities, nations, and organizations have sought to memorialize the fallen through a variety of means, from monuments and memorials to commemorative ceremonies and cultural expressions.

11.1.1 The Human Toll:

World War II exacted a staggering toll on human life, with an estimated 70 to 85 million people perishing as a direct result of the conflict. Among them were millions of military personnel from all branches of service, as well as civilians caught in the crossfire of battle, bombing raids, and genocide. The loss of life was felt keenly by families, communities, and nations, leaving behind a legacy of grief, mourning, and remembrance that endures to this day.

11.1.2 Honoring the Fallen:

The act of honoring the fallen takes many forms, ranging from simple gestures of remembrance to elaborate monuments and memorials. In towns and cities around the world, cenotaphs, war memorials, and honor rolls serve as tangible reminders of the sacrifices made by local residents who served in World War II. These monuments often bear the names of the fallen, ensuring that their memory lives on for future generations.

11.1.3 Personal Tributes:

In addition to public memorials, individuals and families have found their own ways to honor the memory of loved ones who served in World War II. Personal tributes such as photographs, letters, diaries, and keepsakes serve as tangible reminders of the lives lost and the sacrifices made by those who served.

Family members may also visit gravesites, lay flowers, and observe moments of silence to pay their respects and honor the memory of the fallen.

11.2 The Establishment of National Monuments and Memorials:

In the years following World War II, nations around the world began to establish national monuments and memorials to commemorate the sacrifices of those who served. These monuments serve as solemn reminders of the human cost of war and as symbols of national unity, resilience, and sacrifice.

11.2.1 The National World War II Memorial (United States):

In the United States, the National World War II Memorial stands as a testament to the bravery and sacrifice of the more than 16 million Americans who served in the war. Located on the National Mall in Washington, D.C., the memorial features granite pillars, bronze bas-reliefs, and a central fountain, all surrounded by a plaza adorned with bronze wreaths and inscriptions honoring the service and sacrifice of Americans during World War II.

11.2.2 The Cenotaph (United Kingdom):

In the United Kingdom, the Cenotaph in London's Whitehall serves as the focal point for national remembrance ceremonies and commemorations. Originally built to honor the fallen of World War I, the Cenotaph was later expanded to include the names of those who died in World War II and subsequent conflicts. Each year, on Remembrance Sunday, veterans, dignitaries, and members of the public gather at the Cenotaph to pay their respects and observe a two-minute silence in honor of the fallen.

11.2.3 The Yasukuni Shrine (Japan):

In Japan, the Yasukuni Shrine in Tokyo serves as a controversial memorial to the country's war dead, including those who served in World War II. The shrine houses the souls of more than 2.4 million individuals who died in service to Japan, including soldiers, sailors, and airmen from World War II and other conflicts. Visits to the Yasukuni Shrine by Japanese politicians and dignitaries have often sparked controversy and diplomatic tensions with neighboring countries due to its association with Japan's militaristic past.

11.2.4 The Shrine of Remembrance (Australia):

In Australia, the Shrine of Remembrance in Melbourne stands as a solemn tribute to the men and women of Victoria who served in World War II and other conflicts. The shrine features classical architecture, symbolic sculptures, and a central sanctuary with an eternal flame, all surrounded by tranquil gardens and reflective spaces. Each year, on Anzac Day and Remembrance Day, Australians gather at the shrine to honor the memory of the fallen and pay their respects to those who served.

11.3 Commemoration Ceremonies:

Commemoration ceremonies play a central role in honoring the memory of those who served in World War II and ensuring that their sacrifices are never forgotten. These ceremonies bring together veterans, dignitaries, and members of the public to pay tribute to the fallen and reflect on the lessons of the past.

11.3.1 Remembrance Day (United Kingdom):

In the United Kingdom, Remembrance Day, observed on November 11th, commemorates the end of World War I and honors the memory of all those who have died in service to the nation. The day is marked by solemn ceremonies, including two minutes of silence at 11:00 a.m. to remember the fallen. Poppy wreaths are laid at war memorials across the country, and services of remembrance are held in churches, cathedrals, and public spaces. The annual Remembrance Sunday service at the Cenotaph in London is a focal point of national commemoration, attended by members of the royal family, government officials, military leaders, and representatives of veteran organizations.

11.3.2 Anzac Day (Australia and New Zealand):

Anzac Day, observed on April 25th, commemorates the landing of Australian and New Zealand troops at Gallipoli during World War I and honors the service and sacrifice of all Australian and New Zealand military personnel. The day begins with dawn services at war memorials and cenotaphs across both countries, followed by marches, wreath-laying ceremonies, and commemorative events throughout the day. Anzac Day holds special significance in the national consciousness of Australia and New Zealand, symbolizing the spirit of courage, mateship, and sacrifice that defines the Anzac legacy.

11.3.3 Veterans Day (United States):

In the United States, Veterans Day, observed on November 11th, honors military veterans who have served in the Armed Forces. Originally known as Armistice Day to commemorate the end of World War I, the holiday was later expanded to honor veterans of all wars. Veterans Day is marked by ceremonies, parades, and observances in communities across the country, as well as wreath-laying ceremonies at national cemeteries and war memorials. It is a time to express gratitude to veterans for their service and sacrifice and to reflect on the enduring legacy of their contributions to the nation.

11.3.4 Victory Day (Russia):

In Russia and other former Soviet states, Victory Day, observed on May 9th, commemorates the surrender of Nazi Germany to the Soviet Union in 1945 and the end of World War II in Europe. Victory Day is celebrated with elaborate ceremonies, military parades, and public festivities, including fireworks, concerts, and cultural events. It is a time to honor the memory of the millions of Soviet soldiers and civilians who perished in the war and to pay tribute to their courage, resilience, and sacrifice in the fight against fascism and tyranny.

11.4 The Cultural Legacy of World War II:

The legacy of World War II extends far beyond the battlefield, shaping the cultural landscape of nations around the world and leaving an indelible mark on literature, art, film, music, and popular culture.

11.4.1 Literature:

World War II has inspired countless works of literature, ranging from memoirs and historical accounts to novels and poetry. Authors such as Ernest Hemingway, Kurt Vonnegut, Anne Frank, and Elie Wiesel have captured the human experience of war with haunting clarity and emotional resonance, exploring themes of heroism, sacrifice, trauma, and resilience. Their works continue to resonate with readers, offering insights into the complexities of war and its impact on the human spirit.

11.4.2 Art:

Artists have long grappled with the horrors of war, using their creativity to bear witness to the suffering and loss experienced by millions of people during World War II. Painters, sculptors, photographers, and other visual artists have depicted the devastation of war, the courage of soldiers, and the resilience of civilians with depth, sensitivity, and compassion. Works such as Picasso's "Guernica," Goya's "The Disasters of War," and Eisenstein's "Alexander Nevsky" have become iconic symbols of the human cost of conflict and the enduring power of art to evoke empathy and understanding.

11.4.3 Film:

World War II has been a perennial subject of cinema, inspiring filmmakers to tell stories of heroism, sacrifice, love, and loss on the big screen. Classic films such as "Casablanca," "Saving Private Ryan," "Schindler's List," and "The Bridge on the River Kwai" have captured the imagination of audiences around the world, offering powerful narratives of courage, redemption, and the human spirit in the face of adversity. These films continue to resonate with viewers, reminding us of the enduring legacy of World War II and the lessons we can learn from its history.

11.4.4 Music:

Music has played a central role in commemorating the sacrifices of those who served in World War II, with songs such as "We'll Meet Again," "The White Cliffs of Dover," and "Lili Marleen" becoming anthems of hope, resilience, and remembrance. Musicians and composers have drawn inspiration from the wartime experience to create music that reflects the struggles, triumphs, and losses of the era, from the stirring patriotic melodies of the Big Band era to the haunting ballads of the Holocaust and the resistance movements. These songs continue to resonate with listeners, serving as a reminder of the enduring power of music to heal, inspire, and unite people in times of crisis.

11.5 Conclusion:

The memory of World War II lives on in the hearts and minds of people around the world, as we continue to honor the sacrifices of those who served and commemorate the legacy of their contributions to peace, freedom, and democracy. Through monuments and memorials, commemoration ceremonies, and cultural expressions, we pay tribute to the fallen and ensure that their memory lives on for future generations to learn from and remember. National monuments and memorials serve as solemn reminders of the human cost of war, while commemoration ceremonies provide opportunities for reflection and tribute. The cultural legacy of World War II, reflected in literature, art, film, and music, helps us to understand the experiences of those who lived through the war and its aftermath.

As we remember the fallen, we also honor their courage, resilience, and sacrifice. Their legacy is not only a testament to the human spirit in times of adversity but also a reminder of the importance of preserving peace and preventing future conflicts. By commemorating their memory and learning from the lessons of the past, we strive to build a better future for generations to come. Through our ecollectiveefforts to remember the fallen, we ensure that their sacrifices will never be forgotten and that their spirit will continue to inspire us to strive for a world of peace, justice, and understanding.

Chapter 12: The Cold War Begins

The end of World War II marked the beginning of a new era in global politics, characterized by the emergence of the United States and the Soviet Union as superpowers and the onset of the Cold War. This chapter delves into the complex dynamics that shaped this period, including tensions over post-war reconstruction, the division of Europe, and the ominous specter of nuclear weapons and mutually assured destruction.

12.1 The Emergence of Superpowers:

Following the conclusion of World War II, the United States and the Soviet Union emerged as the dominant powers on the world stage, each wielding considerable economic, political, and military influence. While they had been allies during the war, their ideological differences and geopolitical ambitions soon set them on a collision course, laying the groundwork for the Cold War.

12.1.1 The United States:

The United States emerged from World War II as the preeminent economic and military power, boasting a robust industrial base, a thriving economy, and unrivaled military capabilities. With the defeat of Nazi Germany and Imperial Japan, the United States positioned itself as a champion of democracy, freedom, and liberal values, seeking to promote its vision of a post-war world order based on international cooperation, free trade, and collective security.

12.1.2 The Soviet Union:

The Soviet Union, under the leadership of Joseph Stalin, emerged from World War II as a formidable military and political force, having borne the brunt of the fighting on the Eastern Front and suffered immense human and material losses. Despite the devastation wrought by the war, the Soviet Union emerged as a superpower with a vast territory, a powerful military, and a fervent commitment to spreading communism and asserting its influence in Eastern Europe and beyond.

12.2 Tensions over Post-War Reconstruction:

The aftermath of World War II saw tensions between the United States and the Soviet Union over the reconstruction of war-torn Europe and the future of the continent. While the two powers had been allies in the fight against fascism, their divergent visions for post-war Europe soon led to a breakdown in relations and the onset of the Cold War.

12.2.1 The Division of Europe:

One of the key sources of tension between the United States and the Soviet Union was the division of Europe into Western and Eastern spheres of influence. In the West, the United States and its allies sought to promote democracy, economic liberalization, and integration through initiatives such as the Marshall Plan and the formation of NATO (North Atlantic Treaty Organization). In the East, the Soviet Union sought to establish communist regimes and extend its control over Eastern European countries through a combination of military occupation, political manipulation, and ideological indoctrination.

12.2.2 The Iron Curtain:

The division of Europe was symbolized by the "Iron Curtain," a term coined by British Prime Minister Winston Churchill to describe the ideological and physical barrier that separated Western Europe from Eastern Europe. The Iron Curtain represented not only the division of the continent but also the ideological divide between the capitalist West and the communist East, as well as the growing militarization and polarization of the Cold War.

12.3 The Beginning of the Nuclear Arms Race:

One of the defining features of the Cold War was the nuclear arms race between the United States and the Soviet Union, which began in earnest in the aftermath of World War II. The development and proliferation of nuclear weapons raised the stakes of the Cold War, introducing the specter of mutually assured destruction and the possibility of catastrophic global conflict.

12.3.1 The Manhattan Project:

The nuclear arms race began with the development of atomic weapons during World War II, culminating in the successful test of the first atomic bomb by the United States in July 1945. The Manhattan Project, the top-secret research and development effort to build the atomic bomb, involved thousands of scientists, engineers, and workers, and resulted in the creation of two atomic bombs that were dropped on the Japanese cities of Hiroshima and Nagasaki in August 1945, hastening the end of the war.

12.3.2 The Soviet Atomic Bomb:

The United States' monopoly on nuclear weapons was short-lived, as the Soviet Union successfully tested its own atomic bomb in 1949, much to the shock and dismay of the Western powers. The Soviet Union's entry into the nuclear club marked the beginning of the nuclear arms race in earnest, as both superpowers raced to develop more powerful and sophisticated nuclear weapons, delivery systems, and defense capabilities.

12.3.3 Mutually Assured Destruction:

The doctrine of mutually assured destruction (MAD) emerged as a central tenet of nuclear deterrence during the Cold War, positing that the threat of nuclear annihilation would deter both sides from initiating a nuclear conflict. According to MAD theory, the sheer destructiveness of nuclear weapons and the certainty of retaliation would make any nuclear war unwinnable and therefore unthinkable, thus serving as a deterrent to aggression and conflict between nuclear-armed states.

12.4 Conclusion:

The Cold War was a period of intense geopolitical rivalry, ideological confrontation, and military brinkmanship between the United States and the Soviet Union, characterized by the emergence of two superpowers and the onset of the nuclear arms race. Tensions over post-war reconstruction, the division of Europe, and the proliferation of nuclear weapons fueled mistrust, suspicion, and hostility between the two powers, setting the stage for decades of confrontation and competition for global supremacy. As the Cold War unfolded, the world found itself locked in a precarious balance of power, teetering on the brink of nuclear catastrophe while striving to maintain peace and stability in an increasingly volatile and uncertain world. The emergence of the United States and the Soviet Union as superpowers reshaped the geopolitical landscape, with profound implications for global security, diplomacy, and international relations.

12.4.1 Geopolitical Shifts:

The Cold War brought about significant shifts in the geopolitical balance of power, as the United States and the Soviet Union vied for influence and control over strategic regions and resources around the world. Proxy conflicts and regional rivalries played out in places such as Korea, Vietnam, and the Middle East, as both superpowers sought to advance their interests and contain the spread of communism or capitalism.

12.4.2 Ideological Divide:

At the heart of the Cold War was the ideological divide between capitalism and communism, democracy and totalitarianism. The United States championed the principles of freedom, democracy, and free-market capitalism, while the Soviet Union espoused the ideals of socialism, collectivism, and state-controlled economy. This ideological rivalry fueled competition and conflict across multiple fronts, from political propaganda and cultural exchanges to military alliances and proxy wars.

12.4.3 Arms Race and Detente:

Throughout the Cold War, the United States and the Soviet Union engaged in a dangerous and costly arms race, stockpiling nuclear weapons and developing ever more sophisticated delivery systems and defense technologies. The proliferation of nuclear weapons raised the specter of global annihilation and posed an existential threat to humanity. However, efforts to mitigate tensions and reduce the risk of nuclear war also led to periods of detente, characterized by diplomatic dialogue, arms control negotiations, and confidence-building measures aimed at easing tensions and promoting stability.

12.4.4 Legacy of the Cold War:

The Cold War left a lasting legacy that continues to shape global politics and security dynamics to this day. While the collapse of the Soviet Union in 1991 marked the end of the Cold War era, its legacy lingers in ongoing geopolitical rivalries, regional conflicts, and nuclear proliferation challenges. The lessons learned from the Cold War, including the dangers of ideological extremism, the imperative of diplomacy and dialogue, and the importance of arms control and non-proliferation efforts, remain relevant in today's world.

12.5 Conclusion:

The beginning of the Cold War marked a watershed moment in modern history, as the world witnessed the emergence of two superpowers locked in a struggle for global supremacy. Tensions over post-war reconstruction, the division of Europe, and the nuclear arms race defined the contours of the Cold War era, shaping the course of international relations and the destiny of nations. As the United States and the Soviet Union navigated the treacherous waters of geopolitical rivalry and ideological confrontation, the world stood on the brink of nuclear catastrophe, yet also held out hope for peace, cooperation, and collective security. As we reflect on the legacy of the Cold War, we are reminded of the enduring importance of dialogue, diplomacy, and cooperation in addressing the complex challenges of the 21st century and building a more peaceful and prosperous world for future generations.

Chapter 13: Lessons Learned

As the dust settled on the battlefields of World War II and the world grappled with the devastation and loss left in its wake, profound lessons emerged that continue to resonate with humanity to this day. In this chapter, we reflect on America's role in World War II, explore the moral and ethical considerations in warfare, and examine the lasting legacy of the war in shaping American identity and foreign policy.

13.1 Reflections on America's Role in World War II:

America's entry into World War II marked a pivotal moment in the conflict, shifting the balance of power and ultimately leading to the defeat of the Axis powers. As we reflect on America's role in the war, several key lessons emerge:

13.1.1 The Power of Unity:

One of the most striking aspects of America's involvement in World War II was the unprecedented level of national unity and mobilization that occurred. The war effort brought together Americans from all walks of life, transcending political, social, and cultural divides in pursuit of a common goal. From the factories of the industrial heartland to the battlefields of Europe and the Pacific, Americans rallied behind the cause of freedom and democracy, demonstrating the power of collective action in the face of adversity.

13.1.2 The Cost of War:

World War II exacted a heavy toll on America and its allies, both in terms of human lives lost and economic resources expended. The sacrifices made by American servicemen and women, as well as their families, are a sobering reminder of the true cost of war. As we reflect on the immense human suffering and loss experienced during the conflict, we are reminded of the importance of seeking diplomatic solutions to international disputes and striving to prevent the outbreak of future conflicts through dialogue and negotiation.

13.1.3 The Imperative of Leadership:

America's leadership role in World War II demonstrated the importance of strong and decisive leadership in times of crisis. From President Franklin D. Roosevelt's steady hand in guiding the nation through the early years of the war to General Dwight D. Eisenhower's strategic acumen in planning the D-Day invasion, effective leadership played a critical role in shaping the outcome of the conflict. As we reflect on the lessons of World War II, we are reminded of the importance of leadership in promoting peace, stability, and cooperation on the world stage.

13.2 Moral and Ethical Considerations in Warfare:

The conduct of warfare raises profound moral and ethical questions that continue to challenge societies and policymakers to this day. As we examine the moral and ethical considerations in warfare, several key lessons emerge:

13.2.1 The Sanctity of Human Life:

One of the fundamental principles of ethical warfare is the recognition of the inherent value and dignity of human life. The indiscriminate targeting of civilians, the use of weapons of mass destruction, and the commission of atrocities and war crimes violate this principle and undermine the moral legitimacy of armed conflict. As we reflect on the horrors of World War II, including the Holocaust, the firebombing of cities, and the dropping of atomic bombs, we are reminded of the need to uphold the sanctity of human life and to ensure that the conduct of warfare is governed by principles of justice, proportionality, and respect for basic human rights.

13.2.2 The Principle of Just War:

The concept of just war, rooted in moral and theological traditions, provides a framework for evaluating the ethical justification for the use of military force. According to the principles of just war theory, military action must meet certain criteria, including the presence of a just cause, a legitimate authority to wage war, a reasonable prospect of success, and a commitment to minimizing harm to non-combatants. As we reflect on America's role in World War II, we are challenged to consider whether the war met these criteria and whether the means employed were proportionate to the ends sought.

13.2.3 The Responsibility to Protect:

The principle of the responsibility to protect (R2P) asserts that states have a moral and legal obligation to protect their populations from genocide, war crimes, ethnic cleansing, and crimes against humanity. When states fail to fulfill this responsibility, the international community has a duty to intervene, including through the use of military force if necessary, to prevent or halt mass atrocities. As we reflect on the lessons of World War II, including the failure to prevent the Holocaust and other atrocities, we are reminded of the importance of upholding the responsibility to protect and of the need for collective action to prevent future humanitarian crises.

13.3 The Legacy of the War in Shaping American Identity and Foreign Policy:

World War II left an indelible mark on American society and foreign policy, shaping the nation's identity, values, and worldview in profound ways. As we examine the legacy of the war, several key lessons emerge:

13.3.1 The Emergence of the United States as a Global Power:

World War II catapulted the United States onto the world stage as a preeminent economic, military, and political power. The defeat of the Axis powers and the subsequent reconstruction of Europe and Japan cemented America's role as a leader of the free world, committed to promoting democracy, prosperity, and security on a global scale. As we reflect on America's role in World War II, we are reminded of the responsibilities that come with global leadership and of the need to exercise power responsibly and in accordance with principles of justice and democracy.

13.3.2 The Promotion of Liberal Internationalism:

The experience of World War II reinforced the principles of liberal internationalism in American foreign policy, emphasizing the importance of international cooperation, multilateralism, and collective security in addressing global challenges. The creation of institutions such as the United Nations, the World Bank, and the International Monetary Fund reflected America's commitment to fostering a rules-based international order and promoting peace, stability, and prosperity around the world.

13.3.3 The Commitment to Human Rights and Democracy:

The atrocities committed during World War II, including the Holocaust and other mass atrocities, galvanized global efforts to promote human rights and democracy as fundamental principles of international relations. The adoption of the Universal Declaration of Human Rights in 1948, with strong support from the United States, underscored the commitment of the international community to upholding the inherent dignity and rights of all individuals, regardless of race, religion, or nationality. As we reflect on the legacy of the war, we are reminded of the ongoing struggle to protect and advance human rights and democracy in an ever-changing world.

13.3.4 The Pursuit of Pax Americana:

In the aftermath of World War II, the United States emerged as the primary guarantor of global security and stability, seeking to maintain a Pax Americana characterized by peace, prosperity, and freedom. Through alliances such as NATO and regional security partnerships, the United States sought to contain the spread of communism, deter aggression, and promote stability in key strategic regions around the world. As we reflect on America's role in World War II, we are challenged to consider the enduring legacy of Pax Americana and its implications for the future of international relations.

13.4 Conclusion:

As we reflect on the lessons learned from World War II, we are reminded of the enduring importance of striving for peace, justice, and human dignity in a world fraught with conflict and uncertainty. The war taught us the importance of unity, leadership, and moral courage in confronting the challenges of our time, and it underscored the imperative of upholding the principles of just war and the responsibility to protect in the conduct of international affairs. As we look to the future, we must heed the lessons of the past and remain vigilant in our efforts to build a more peaceful, prosperous, and just world for generations to come.

Chapter 14: Continuing Impact

The echoes of World War II continue to reverberate through the corridors of history, shaping politics, culture, and society in profound ways. In this chapter, we delve into the ongoing influence of World War II on the modern world, America's role in promoting democracy and human rights, and the enduring challenges and conflicts that persist in the post-war era.

14.1 The Ongoing Influence of World War II:

Nearly eight decades after the end of World War II, its impact continues to be felt across the globe. From the political landscape to the cultural zeitgeist, the war has left an indelible mark on the modern world, shaping the course of history in myriad ways.

14.1.1 Political Legacy:

World War II fundamentally altered the geopolitical landscape, redrawing borders, reshaping alliances, and realigning global power dynamics. The emergence of the United States and the Soviet Union as superpowers, the establishment of the United Nations, and the division of Europe into Eastern and Western blocs are among the lasting political legacies of the war. The Cold War rivalry between the United States and the Soviet Union, fueled by ideological differences and geopolitical ambitions, dominated international relations for much of the 20th century and continues to influence global politics to this day.

14.1.2 Economic Impact:

The economic consequences of World War II were far-reaching, as nations grappled with the immense costs of war and the challenges of post-war reconstruction. The war accelerated technological innovation, spurred industrial growth, and transformed global trade patterns. In the aftermath of the war, the United States emerged as the world's leading economic power, driving the post-war recovery and shaping the contours of the international economic order. The Marshall Plan, a massive aid program launched by the United States to rebuild war-torn Europe, laid the foundation for European integration and economic prosperity, while also cementing America's role as a global economic leader.

14.1.3 Cultural Legacy:

World War II has left an enduring imprint on the cultural landscape, inspiring countless works of literature, art, film, and music that continue to captivate and resonate with audiences around the world. From the harrowing accounts of Holocaust survivors to the heroic tales of Allied soldiers, the war has provided fertile ground for artistic expression and exploration. Films such as "Schindler's List," "Saving Private Ryan," and "The Pianist," novels such as "Night" by Elie Wiesel and "The Diary of Anne Frank," and artworks such as Picasso's "Guernica" have become iconic symbols of the human experience of war and the struggle for survival, resilience, and hope.

14.2 America's Role in Promoting Democracy and Human Rights:

Throughout its history, the United States has played a central role in advancing the cause of democracy and human rights around the world. The lessons learned from World War II, including the horrors of totalitarianism and the importance of freedom and justice, have shaped America's foreign policy and its commitment to promoting democracy, human rights, and the rule of law.

14.2.1 The Spread of Democracy:

In the aftermath of World War II, the United States emerged as a champion of democracy, seeking to foster the spread of democratic ideals and institutions in regions ravaged by war and oppression. Through initiatives such as the Marshall Plan, the Truman Doctrine, and the establishment of institutions such as NATO and the United Nations, the United States sought to promote stability, prosperity, and democracy in Europe and beyond. The collapse of the Soviet Union and the spread of democracy in Eastern Europe in the late 20th century are testament to the enduring impact of America's commitment to democratic values and principles.

14.2.2 The Promotion of Human Rights:

World War II brought to light the atrocities committed by totalitarian regimes and underscored the importance of protecting human rights and dignity. In the aftermath of the war, the United States played a leading role in advocating for the universal recognition of human rights and the establishment of international norms and standards to safeguard fundamental freedoms. The adoption of the Universal Declaration of Human Rights in 1948, with strong support from the United States, marked a milestone in the global struggle for human rights and served as a rallying cry for oppressed peoples around the world. From the Civil Rights Movement at home to the fight against apartheid in South

Africa, the United States has stood at the forefront of the struggle for human rights and equality, inspiring generations of activists and advocates to champion the cause of justice and dignity for all.

14.3 Challenges and Conflicts in the Post-war Era:

Despite the end of World War II, the world continues to grapple with a myriad of challenges and conflicts that have their roots in the aftermath of the war. From the rise of authoritarian regimes to the proliferation of nuclear weapons, the post-war era has been marked by persistent threats to peace, stability, and prosperity.

14.3.1 The Cold War Legacy:

The legacy of the Cold War continues to shape global politics and security dynamics, as the world contends with the enduring legacy of superpower rivalry, nuclear proliferation, and regional conflicts. While the collapse of the Soviet Union brought an end to the Cold War era, its legacy continues to manifest in renewed great power competition, geopolitical tensions, and proxy conflicts in regions such as the Middle East, Eastern Europe, and Asia. The ongoing conflict in Ukraine, the nuclear ambitions of North Korea, and the rise of authoritarianism in countries such as Russia and China are among the challenges that stem from the Cold War legacy.

14.3.2 Terrorism and Extremism:

The post-war era has also seen the rise of terrorism and extremism as significant threats to global peace and security. From the attacks of September 11, 2001, to the rise of ISIS in the Middle East, terrorist organizations have exploited political, social, and economic grievances to sow chaos and violence around the world. The fight against terrorism remains a pressing challenge for the international community, requiring concerted efforts to address the root causes of extremism, strengthen counterterrorism capabilities, and promote stability and development in conflict-affected regions.

14.3.3 Global Challenges:

In addition to traditional security threats, the post-war era has also brought to the forefront a range of global challenges that require collective action and cooperation to address. Issues such as climate change, pandemics, mass migration, and economic inequality pose existential threats to humanity and require innovative solutions and concerted efforts from the international community.

14.3.4 Climate Change:

Climate change, driven by human activities such as deforestation, industrialization, and the burning of fossil fuels, poses a grave threat to the planet's ecosystems, biodiversity, and human societies. Rising temperatures, extreme weather events, sea-level rise, and environmental degradation are already having profound impacts on vulnerable communities around the world, exacerbating poverty, food insecurity, and displacement. Addressing climate change requires ambitious action to reduce greenhouse gas emissions, transition to renewable energy sources, and build resilience to climate impacts, as well as international cooperation to support mitigation and adaptation efforts in developing countries.

14.3.5 Pandemics:

The COVID-19 pandemic, which swept across the globe in 2020, underscored the interconnectedness of the modern world and the vulnerabilities inherent in our globalized societies. The pandemic highlighted the importance of robust public health systems, coordinated international responses, and equitable access to vaccines and medical treatments. It also exposed disparities in healthcare access and socioeconomic inequality, exacerbating existing inequalities and vulnerabilities. As the world continues to grapple with the COVID-19 pandemic and prepares for future health crises, strengthening global health governance, investing in pandemic preparedness and response capabilities, and promoting cooperation and solidarity are essential for safeguarding public health and well-being.

14.3.6 Mass Migration:

Mass migration, driven by factors such as conflict, persecution, economic hardship, and environmental degradation, has become a defining feature of the post-war era. Displacement crises in regions such as Syria, Afghanistan, and South Sudan have forced millions of people to flee their homes in search of safety and opportunity, straining resources, exacerbating tensions, and testing the capacity of countries and communities to respond. Addressing the root causes of displacement, protecting the rights of refugees and migrants, and fostering inclusive and sustainable development are essential for managing migration flows and addressing the humanitarian and security challenges associated with displacement.

14.3.7 Economic Inequality:

Despite significant progress in reducing poverty and improving living standards in many parts of the world, economic inequality remains a pervasive and persistent challenge. The gap between the rich and the poor, both within and between countries, continues to widen, exacerbating social tensions, undermining social cohesion, and limiting opportunities for economic mobility and upward social mobility. Addressing economic inequality requires a comprehensive approach that includes progressive taxation, social safety nets, investment in education and healthcare, and inclusive economic growth strategies that prioritize the needs of marginalized and vulnerable populations.

14.4 Conclusion:

As we reflect on the continuing impact of World War II, we are reminded of the enduring relevance of its lessons and legacies in shaping the modern world. From the promotion of democracy and human rights to the challenges and conflicts that persist in the post-war era, the war continues to shape politics, culture, and society in profound ways. As we confront the pressing challenges of our time, from climate change and pandemics to economic inequality and mass migration, we must draw upon the lessons learned from World War II and work together to build a more peaceful, prosperous, and just world for future generations. Through collective action, cooperation, and solidarity, we can overcome the challenges of the present and chart a course towards a better, more sustainable future for all.

Chapter 15: The Enduring Legacy

As we reach the conclusion of our exploration of World War II and its profound impact on America and the world, it is essential to reflect on the enduring legacy of the war, the importance of remembering and learning from history, and the role of America in shaping global events both past and future.

15.1 The Lasting Impact of World War II on America and the World:

World War II left an indelible mark on both America and the world, shaping the course of history and profoundly influencing politics, culture, and society in the decades that followed.

15.1.1 Political Legacy:

The political legacy of World War II is evident in the emergence of the United States as a global superpower and the establishment of a new world order based on principles of democracy, human rights, and collective security. The defeat of fascism and the triumph of liberal democracy reaffirmed America's commitment to promoting freedom and democracy around the world, laying the foundation for the post-war era of Pax Americana and the spread of democratic ideals and institutions.

15.1.2 Cultural Impact:

The cultural impact of World War II is evident in the enduring legacy of literature, art, film, and music that emerged from the war. From the haunting memoirs of Holocaust survivors to the iconic imagery of Allied victory, the war has inspired countless works of creative expression that continue to resonate with audiences around the world. Films such as "Casablanca," "Schindler's List," and "Saving Private Ryan," novels such as "Catch-22" and "Slaughterhouse-Five," and artworks such as Picasso's "Guernica" have become touchstones of the human experience of war and the struggle for survival, resilience, and hope.

15.1.3 Social Transformation:

World War II brought about significant social transformation, both in America and abroad. The war accelerated the pace of social change, breaking down barriers of race, gender, and class and expanding opportunities for marginalized and underrepresented groups. The wartime mobilization effort opened up new avenues of employment for women and minorities, challenging traditional gender roles and paving the way for greater social equality and inclusion. The experience of war also fostered a sense of national unity and solidarity, as Americans of all backgrounds came together in common cause to defend freedom and democracy.

15.2 Reflections on the Importance of Remembering and Learning from History:

As we reflect on the enduring legacy of World War II, it is essential to recognize the importance of remembering and learning from history. The lessons of the war—about the dangers of totalitarianism, the horrors of war, and the resilience of the human spirit—remain relevant today and serve as a sobering reminder of the fragility of peace and the dangers of intolerance and extremism.

15.2.1 Preserving Memory:

Preserving the memory of World War II is essential for honoring the sacrifices of those who served and ensuring that the lessons of the past are not forgotten. Memorials, museums, and commemoration ceremonies play a crucial role in preserving the memory of the war and educating future generations about its significance. From the National World War II Memorial in Washington, D.C., to the Holocaust Memorial Museum in Jerusalem, these institutions serve as powerful reminders of the human cost of war and the importance of striving for peace and justice.

15.2.2 Learning from History:

Learning from history is essential for avoiding the mistakes of the past and building a better future. The lessons of World War II—about the dangers of nationalism, the importance of diplomacy, and the imperative of international cooperation—are as relevant today as they were during the war. By studying the causes and consequences of the war, we gain valuable insights into the complexities of human nature and the challenges of navigating a world fraught with conflict and uncertainty.

15.3 Looking Towards the Future and the Role of America in Shaping Global Events:

As we look towards the future, it is essential to consider the role of America in shaping global events and addressing the challenges of the 21st century. As a global superpower with immense economic, military, and diplomatic capabilities, America has a unique responsibility to lead by example and promote peace, prosperity, and democracy around the world.

15.3.1 Global Leadership:

America's leadership on the world stage is essential for addressing pressing global challenges such as climate change, pandemics, terrorism, and nuclear proliferation. By working collaboratively with allies and partners, upholding democratic values and human rights, and championing multilateralism and international cooperation, America can help to build a more peaceful, prosperous, and just world for all.

15.3.2 Diplomatic Engagement:

Diplomatic engagement is crucial for resolving conflicts, preventing crises, and advancing America's interests and values on the world stage. By engaging in dialogue and negotiation with adversaries, promoting conflict resolution and reconciliation, and upholding the principles of diplomacy and dialogue, America can help to de-escalate tensions, build trust, and foster stability in regions of strategic importance.

15.3.3 Economic Prosperity:

Economic prosperity is essential for promoting stability, reducing poverty, and addressing the root causes of conflict and insecurity. By fostering economic growth, expanding trade and investment opportunities, and promoting inclusive and sustainable development, America can help to create the conditions for peace and prosperity to thrive.

15.3.4 Promoting Democracy and Human Rights:

Promoting democracy and human rights is central to America's identity and values as a nation. By supporting democratic transitions, defending human rights defenders, and holding authoritarian regimes accountable for their abuses, America can help to advance freedom, justice, and dignity for all people around the world.

15.4 Conclusion:

As we conclude our exploration of the enduring legacy of World War II, we are reminded of the profound impact of the war on America and the world and the importance of remembering and learning from history. By preserving the memory of the war, learning from its lessons, and looking towards the future with hope and determination, we can honor the sacrifices of those who served and build a better world for future generations. As America continues to navigate the complexities of the 21st century, its leadership and engagement on the world stage will be essential for promoting peace, prosperity, and democracy and shaping a brighter future for all.

Don't miss out!

Visit the website below and you can sign up to receive emails whenever Michael Johnson publishes a new book. There's no charge and no obligation.

https://books2read.com/r/B-A-OREFB-BYWZC

Did you love *World War II*? Then you should read *American Chronicles*[1] by Michael Johnson!

[2]

"American Chronicles: A History of the United States" offers a comprehensive journey through the pivotal moments that shaped the nation. From the rich tapestry of indigenous civilizations to the tumultuous struggles of the Civil Rights Movement and beyond, this book explores the key events, figures, and themes that define American history. From the Revolutionary War to the Cold War and beyond, witness the rise of a nation, the trials of war, and the ongoing quest for equality and freedom. Experience the story of America, from its origins to its enduring legacy in the modern world.

---

1. https://books2read.com/u/3y9qLL

2. https://books2read.com/u/3y9qLL

About the Author

Michael Johnson is a distinguished historian specializing in American history. With a degree in History from Harvard University, Johnson's work delves into pivotal moments, figures, and themes shaping the United States. He has authored numerous acclaimed books, offering insightful perspectives and engaging narratives. Johnson's commitment to meticulous scholarship and compelling storytelling has earned him widespread acclaim in the field. Passionate about sharing his expertise, he frequently engages in lectures and public events to foster a deeper appreciation for America's past.